Nappy Girl Kitchen Recipe Book

YVONNE JONES

To order additional copies of this book, contact:
Xlibris
844-714-8691
www.Xlibris.com
Orders@Xlibris.com

ISBN: Softcover   978-1-6641-5700-2
        EBook   978-1-6641-5699-9

Print information available on the last page

Rev. date: 02/08/2021

Contents

Pepperoni hamburger bake

INGREDIENTS

3lbs of thawed hamburger meat
3 packs of 5 oz sliced pepperoni
1 pack of 16oz spaghetti noodles

PREPARATION AND COOKING:

- cook for 20 minutes until done/no pink
- cook full box in 4-quart pot for 10 minutes/drain
- In a bowl mix together:
    - 3lbs of hamburger meat
    - 6 cans of organic tomato sauce
    - 6 tablespoons of garlic powder
    - 2 teaspoons of salt (optional)
    - 2 teaspoons of oregano
    - 2 teaspoons of parsley flakes
- In a deep glass baking dish or baking pan layer ingredients
- Layer bottom of pan with tomato and beef mixture
- Second layer spaghetti noodles
- Third layer pepperoni's as much as you like
- Fourth layer of Mozzarella cheese and shredded mild cheese
- Repeat layers until dish is full
- Bake in oven on 350 degrees for 30 minutes

Crispy fried chicken

INGREDIENTS:

5lbs chicken
2 eggs
2 cups of buttermilk
4 tablespoons of salt (optional)
4 tablespoon of garlic powder
1 brown paper bag
6 cups of flour
48 oz. of vegetable oil

PREPARATION:

- place slits in raw chicken for flavor absorption
- Cover raw chicken in cold water in a bowl with 5 Tablespoons of vinegar over night to clean
- The next day drain water off chicken

COOKING TIME:

- ❖ Turn stove top on medium heat
- ❖ Add 48 ounces of vegetable oil to cast iron Dutch pot, place pot over the medium heat, heat for 20 minutes
- ❖ In a bowl mix eggs and buttermilk
- ❖ Rub salt, and garlic powder into chicken pieces
- ❖ Dip one piece of chicken at a time in egg and buttermilk mixture
- ❖ Then place in bag of flour, roll the top of the bag down to close and shake chicken piece to coat with flour
- ❖ Place chicken in Dutch Pot of grease and allow it to fry, turn chicken over in 7 minutes, when the chicken begins to float and the frying sound dies down the chicken is done! Place done chicken pieces on a rack to drain

Seafood Boil

INGREDIENTS:

5 lbs. of crab legs snow crab legs
6,6oz lobster tails
5lbs of shrimp
4 boxes of private selection white wine & garlic mussels
2 bags of baby potatoes
Carton of eggs (12)
12 ears of corn
12 sticks of butter (you can use more if you like)
4 tablespoons of Creole Seasoning
3 tablespoons of cayenne pepper (optional)
3 tablespoons of onion powder

PREPARATION

- rinse crab legs in cold water
- rinse lobster tails off in cold water
- devein and detail shrimp then rinse in cold water
- rinse cook until tender
- cook eggs in for 9 min in an instant pot, drain once done and fill pot with cold water (do not peel while hot)
- cover corn in water and boil on high heat for 15 minutes
- Melt butter in microwavable bowl in microwave

COOKING:

- In a pot of boiling water over high heat boil crab legs, lobster tails, shrimp and mussels for 25 minutes
- In a large disposable serving dish place all of the cooked meat
- Add cooked corn
- Add peeled eggs
- Add potatoes
- In bowl of butter mix creole seasoning, cayenne pepper, and onion powder stir until mixed well then pour over top of seafood and vegetables then serve
- Serves 6 people

Dream Cole Slaw

INGREDIENTS

1-12oz bag of broccoli slaw
2-tablespoons of mayonnaise (you can use more or less)
1-teaspoon of vinegar
¼ cup of sugar
1-tablespoon of salt
1-chopped onion
1 bag of sharp shredded cheese

- ❖ Mix all ingredients together in a bowl
- ❖ Place in refrigerator for 1 hour
- ❖ Serves 4

Chili Spaghetti

INGREDIENTS:

5lbs of ground beef
½ pack of 16 oz spaghetti noodles
1 can of 14.5 diced tomatoes or chop up 2 fresh tomatoes
3 tablespoons of chili powder
3 tablespoons of garlic powder
1-1.25 oz pack of chili seasoning (mild or hot your choice)
1 tablespoon of salt (optional)
6 oz can of tomato paste
1 can of 14 oz black beans do not drain
1 can of 14 oz pinto or kidney beans (your choice) do not drain

PREPARATION:

Thaw ground beef overnight in a bowl of cold water in the refrigerator, drain water off next day

COOKING

❖ Cook ground beef in pot of water cover ground beef with water cook for 30 minutes over high heat
❖ Once ground beef is done/no pink, drain and rinse with cold water
❖ Cook spaghetti noodles for 15 minutes, drain, rinse with cold water
❖ In a pot add cooked ground hamburger, can of tomatoes (do not drain), tomato paste, chili powder, garlic powder, chili seasoning, beans, and salt, stir until evenly mixed
❖ Bring to a slow boil over low heat
❖ Once ingredients come to a slow boil add spaghetti noodles and turn heat off
❖ Serve hot; serves 6

Fried liver and Onions

INGREDIENTS:

2-16 oz packs of liver
1 teaspoon of salt (optional)
¼ cup of Vegetable oil
1 large sliced onion
1 cup of flour

PREPARATION:

- Thaw liver out in cold water once it is thawed drain water
- Place liver in a large bowl and season with salt
- Place flour in a second bowl

COOKING:

- ❖ In a cast iron frying pan add vegetable oil and turn stovetop on medium heat for 10 minutes
- ❖ Gather liver and batter with flour both sides add to pan
- ❖ Fry liver for 4 minutes on each side
- ❖ Remove from pan set liver on a rack to drain extra grease off
- ❖ Place liver in glass serving dish
- ❖ Add onions to remaining grease in pan Sautee for 5 minutes remove and add on top of liver in glass dish
- ❖ Serves 4

Shrimp and Mussel Scampi

INGREDIENTS:

3-16 oz. boxes of private selection mussels with a wine and butter sauce (best results with this one)
1 box of 16 oz. of spaghetti noodles
1lb of private selection peeled and deveined tiger prawn shrimp
1 cup of shredded parmesan cheese
2 sticks of butter

PREPARATION:

- steam in covered pot as directed on the box
- cook noodles in boiling water over high heat for 15 minutes'/drain rinse with cold water
- cook in skillet for 15 minutes over medium heat tbsp. of olive oil
- melt in microwave until completely melted

COOKING

- ❖ Add shrimp and butter, to mussels in pot over low heat
- ❖ Place noodles on dinner plate
- ❖ On top of noodles add mussel and shrimp mixture with sauce
- ❖ Sprinkle parmesan cheese on top and serve
- ❖ Last sprinkle parsley flakes for color
- ❖ Serves 6

Chocolate Almond Coconut Bars

INGREDIENTS:

- o   1 &1/2 bags of 10 oz. milk, white, dark or bittersweet chocolate chips
- o   Bag of sweet coconut flakes 7oz
- o   Small bag of raw almonds
- o   1 ice tray

PREPARATION:

boil a small pot of water, once water comes to a boil turn temperature down to low till water becomes still from movement. Place chocolate chips in a lager pot to sit on top of pot of hot water. Put top on it and let it sit for 1 hour occasionally stirring chocolate

COOKING:

- ❖   Once chocolate has melted layer bottom of ice tray with chocolate
- ❖   Layer coconut on top of chocolate in ice tray
- ❖   Add almond on top of coconut in ice tray
- ❖   Add chocolate again to top layer
- ❖   Place in refrigerator for 1 hour and then serve
- ❖   Serves 6

Lemon Breakfast Cake

Ingredients
9 large eggs
2 sticks of butter (salted or unsalted)
3 cups of all purpose
2 cups of sugar
1 cup of lemon juice
10 strawberries washed and sliced
Deep cake pan

PREPARATION:

- **In a larger mixing bowl add**
- **3 cups of flour**
- **2 sticks of melted butter**
- **add 2 cups of sugar to bowl and mix with hand mixer until smooth**
- **gently add 1 egg at a time while mixing**
- **then add lemon juice, mix all ingredients until batter is smooth, it will be thick**

COOKING:

- ❖ **Preheat oven on 350 degrees prior to mixing ingredients**
- ❖ **Grease cake pan with 1/3 cup of vegetable oil**
- ❖ **Add cake mixture to cake pan**
- ❖ **Place in oven and cook for 1 hour**
- ❖ **To test cake to see if it is done stick a tooth pick in it. If it comes out smooth the cake is done!**
- ❖ **Once it is done remove from oven and allow to cool then remove from cake pan**
- ❖ **Sprinkle powdered sugar over the top and add sliced strawberries to the side for taste and presentation**

Homemade Beef and Lentil Soup

INGREDIENTS:

16 oz. bag of Lentils
3lbs of hamburger meat
12oz Barilla Jumbo Shells
2 cans of chopped carrots
2 celery stalks chopped
1 cup of spinach

PREPARATION:

- Place beans in large pot covered with water over high heat. Cook for 2 hours, make sure there is lentil juice from the beans left when they are done. This will be keep the soup consistent.
- 5-quart pot filled with water enough to cover meatballs   place over medium heat. Roll meat into 2inch balls place in pot and cook for 2 hours until done all the way through. Drain when done and set aside.
- Fill pot with water over high heat place noodles in water cook for 15 minutes until tender.
- Drain when done and refill pot with cold water and sit aside
- Cook celery with meatballs

COOKING

- ❖ Once lentils, meatballs, and shells are done combine all ingredients including carrots and spinach
- ❖ Add 2 tablespoons of salt (optional)
- ❖ 2 Tablespoons of sugar (optional)
- ❖ Heat on medium heat until spinach withers taste for desired results
- ❖ Serves 8

Inspired by Nappy Girl Kitchen

Nappy Girl Kitchen started on social media to assist youth, and individuals who want to obtain cooking skills on a budget. Nappy Girl Kitchen Recipe Book is a new beginning to share recipes that actually work, fun and flavorful. The recipes are easy and are a great way to bring family, friends and children into the kitchen and learn life skills through cooking. I would like to thank my mamma and daddy Mitchell and Fred Jones for allowing me to be myself and showing me cooking skills from adolescence. I would like to thank my children Savannah Jones and Jovial Lovely for inspiring me to keep pushing no matter what!

Printed in the United States
By Bookmasters